OBSERVE THE LARK

.

OBSERVE
THE
LARK

KATIE
LOUCHHEIM

 Vintage Books
A Division of Random House
New York

FIRST VINTAGE BOOKS EDITION, 1985

Portions of this work have previously appeared in the following publications: *Foreign Service Journal, McCall's, The Vineyard Gazette,* and *The Washingtonian.*

Library of Congress Cataloging in
Publication Data
Louchheim, Katie, 1903-
Observe the lark.
I. Title.
PS3562.08025   1985b   811'.54   84-25748
ISBN 0-394-72930-7 (pbk.)

Typography by J. K. Lambert
Manufactured in the United States of America

FOR DONALD

CONTENTS

HYMN TO A WAYWARD SUMMER

We ask for answers, hang our sense
on every summer's sensuous line;
a butterfly, brown, speckled white,
quite common but for sky-blue bands,
knows where to suck. We talk to a book.

Whatever trembles, wing, stem, leaf,
belongs to a most secret sect.
Certain as the breeze-blown curtain,
promised to birth, decay, absolution,
blooms, turns, torn by wind's solution.

Tidiness is not their passion,
give their love to bees and finches,
write with pink, white, grey-blue, purple,
sign off gold, in fields of gentians.
Compass, yardstick, pen and paper,
you are deaf, your dreams are sterile.
That cricket sings, the apple falls,
we watch, we feast, protect, applaud,
your contours strangle us with scent,
you are a vine, you climb our mind.
Preserve us till we meet again.

PEONIES

The sun came in without knocking, stayed
for tea and a portrait of peonies.
The light of the sun burned the maple trunk white
and the peonies, silenced, stood fragile
in tight scarlet curled leaves.

Out of the web of the real,
with all Plato's idyllic ideal,
I count the sum of the day's broken
hours into lines that forever reveal
the mystique we cajole with our tears and sighs.

We renounce . . . in a thousand midnight cries,
we burn on an altar of polished self,
dismember, despise and worship, make vows
to the Presence, to the king of all skies.

Oh, full-leafed tree, oh, immeasurable sun,
keep your secrets; my portrait can never be done.

FATHER SQUIRREL

Rat cousin, plume tailed,
our maple pleased him,
trunk branch four, tail
and claws carried maple's
leaves, teeth tight,
ran in and out
the dark hole facing
a patch of promising sky.
He made two beds.

Catbirds raced, mockers mocked,
counting cardinals and us
we were ten spectators.

That night rain blasted down,
wolf winds howled, torn bark
lay round the struggle. The storm
turned his children blue,
found curled in leaves, all dead.

His paws pressed in prayer
at the broom burial, he swore
"Bred in the same safe hole
their tails full, their claws
steel ladders, well groomed
they shall be reborn."

The maple and the cardinal
conspired, closed the hole.
The nest was noisy,
difficult to referee.

HYDE PARK

One early April English evening
Spilled purple crocus in my tea;
a man's lips waited in the cup,
sweetened by spring's rash legacy.

SUMMER QUATRAIN

Infinity takes up little space,
blackbirds meet in the self-same place,
an inch fern knows but light and shade,
the dark of night . . . and is unafraid.

THE INDISPENSABLE MAN

Small talk had a bank account, a car,
his dinner coat lapels were just as wide
as the careful smile he took such pride in.
At lunch, he wore old school ties.

He had no party. Dems or Reps,
they came, they went, he stood on steps
of hostess power, the hour always eight.
Fluent in accents, he could celebrate

the rise and fall of nations, small and great.
Protocol and wines, he knew by heart.
Fate, alas, had shaped him for a minor part.
Being a man, and single, raised him to an art.

He could say nothing with artistic flair.
At Washington's posh tables he was there.

A WORTHY WOMAN

Mrs. Philmore upholstered in jersey
facing a ballroom of hot peopled air,
sits nervous, feet sideways under her chair.

Preened to preside, she looms omnipresent.
Grey curls blend with pearls. Matching gloves pat
tips of grey fur. She has notes in her lap.

Her symbols of status are borrowed,
the lectern, the gavel, her platform pride
are props loaned to whoever presides:

even her clumsy mechanical thanks
flutter and fade in the speaker's applause.
She stands adjourned, an unresolved cause.

MARIAN MAKEPIECE

The natives said she belonged in a book
She forbade summer to begin or end without her,
Her smock, wide scarf, small dog, pince-nez,
Gave her that odd suspended look.
Marian Makepiece ratified the season.

In flowing cape she bicycled to the club,
Her clique followed like ducks.
She swam in all weathers, gardened in full view.
Bridge consumed her sundown whims. She played for luck.

One parched summer strangers came to live
next door: Their loud shorts offended,
their honking she could not forgive.
She put up a sign: "Do not blow horn."
When their car ran the dog down, even the strangers cried.

Friends called, friends forgot, he was an ugly dog.
Her garden grew wild, she locked herself in.
Nights she rode her bicycle through thick fog.
One of her group found her cape on the beach,
Her pince-nez, the dog's carefully coiled leash.

DEVIL UNDER
THE DREAMING BED

The whole earth lies awake
husbands call from the moon
saying memos delay dates
making them late for love.

Wives wait, mending pride,
counting up winter's lies.

Dogs lose their buried bones,
bark their masters back home.

Spring tries out her shoes.
The sighs that women wear
wrinkle their eyes.
Tears splash on the ground.
Men mistake them for dew.

THE SENSITIVE ONE

You who are so sensitive,
so finely honed, so favored,
you walk through words,

The trees talk to you,
fiercely dispute their right
to own your silence.

Lush meadows, pleading streams,
lonely paths call you by name,
memorize your footfall.

You close the troubled doors,
withhold judgment.
You were last observed

reforesting, planting a new world.

MAIN STREET SUMMER

The day they moved the old house
summer stood handsome on Main.
the back door hung loose in the breeze;
like a ship, she sailed into trees.

Someone held the mortgage: progress
perhaps, or some uncouth kin.
We were too greedy.

Wanting history, what we got
was the day, bright, radiant, hot
choked with the deeds of unlived lives.

THE SINGING YOUNG

Coming from choir practice,
trailing their whites
on rain-painted brick.

Saturday's doubts, double dates,
bass replying to treble
long straight blonde hopes,

thunder under the tentative mustache,
fast feet in irregular loping.
Girls, you'll get smashed. Boys,

you are not yet men.
This is your fall, your gold and
rust capes, leaves at your feet.

You are an army of
irresponsible Christians,
pledged not to make

our mistakes, believe our legends,
take our advice. Your march is
a dance. You are called

only to sing. Hold that note.

EPHESUS

Today you were in the flowers,
white carpet, yellow-purple fringe,
you could not say or would not
where you would be tomorrow:
studying Sappho's short lyric
or listening to Aristotle who asked
whether virtue can be taught.
Or watching the sunset on the bay
from the scooped-out hills
of Ephesus over fertile slopes
threaded by broom all gold
and absolutely useless.

Have you understood why nothing
is permanent but the sea,
why the earth shreds home and ambitions,
the living who had so deftly built
a paradise overlooking the view.

I remember you with Gibbon
with an armlock on philosophers
dragging me home from empty talk
and asking, did you learn anything?

Have you? Is there knowledge? Music too,
surely? Shall I find you listening to Myra Hess

playing through blitz after blitz
with the antiquities in the British Museum,
normally silent, decorous, safely stowed away.

Where can we talk about salvation?
I'll be so silent you will
never know I'm talking to myself
about the lives we spent in
and out of mistakes and pleasures.
One day you will tell me
why and where and when . . .

THE LESSONS OF CHRISTMAS

Tucked round with spruce
let us light up the night
of our separate wishes,

Let dreams sleep in seasons,
stitched in patterns and reason.
Let songs and all symbols

be ransomed, reincarnate
saved by myths and musicians;
let well-practiced traditions

grace our many-faced lives.

II

OBSERVE THE LARK

Hedgerows in Provence, cathedrals,
Joseph, carved around a corner,
cast divine, yet satisfied
with his role as bit performer.

Joseph's solace, nature's dictas,
meet and speak. Observe the lark;
innocent he improvises,
as did David on his harp.

THE SEEING GLASS

Susceptible to yellow doorways,
street gardens, predictions, old bricks in
London's last light, swimming swans, trees spread
with green furred nuts, fond of words,

all creatures that smile, old ladies
in the grand style, unassuming
dawns, unescorted dews, bare winds,
what I cannot change about you.

A SUMMER LOST

Shadows in old frames
know nothing is quite the same.
The heart runs a risk, must confess

greed. Love is outrageous,
we need one another more
rather than less.

THE RIGGING TO THE FULL MOON

"What's for supper?" the rigging asked the moon.
"Creaky rockers talk of me, my music makes sleep,
your rigging sounds sad," the moon sighed.
The rigging sang, "Twang, twang, twang."

"For supper there's old cloud stew,
moon-gold sophistry," the rigging twanged.
"Females with old tales," the moon replied,
"too far from me, out of tune, too."

The moon captured a robber cloud,
"That's for supper," she sang to the crowd.
The rigging sang her twang, twang, twang,
plucked at her strings. The moon sang loud.

FOR LOUISE BOGAN

If God is dead
as the young man said,
why were we given different pigments,
but to hold each other's hands and minds,
manage each other's seas and plains,
reclaim a difference, discover we're made the same,
unbeknownst, the keepers of his joys and seasons,
of his light, his shadows, and his reasons.

MEMORABLE

The day was on parade
we saw leaves so polished
the sun turned jealous of the shade.

We saw one kind of blue
that startled and outshone
the painter's indigo.

We talked of how mundane
and yet how deep the me and you,
different yet the same.

Memories turn fictitious.
Ours could fade, but now
we hold and own the riches

of our priceless day
tight, and tied,
to keep from now, always.

NIGHT MUSIC

The square root of sky
cannot be measured,
creates its own equation.

Giant pines make music
over water, on indifferent stones.
Secrets stalk the wet grass.

Stars let down ladders,
old streams carry the bass
to a young bird's treble.

Night has its own revels.

FROM THESE HEIGHTS

Long green shadows, low clouds
carry night to the mountains,
as the small dust of my mind
carries a sudden rainbow.

As if I called and you came,
unannounced, after the rain.

TO THE HAPPY WIFE
WITH A FATAL FLAW

A wife who lost her shopping list
like a book without a cover
cannot be read, cannot cook supper . . .
might she not misplace her lover?

RECIPE

What are husbands made of?
Impractical, putting table salt
on the iced walk.
Earnest, putting Genesis
into their heads.

Romantic, putting dream stuff
on their bread.

ALL AROUND US

Fields swarm with wild sweet phlox,
bees suck drunk, upside down,
boats sit on a sapphire box.
Someone holds the sea tight, all around.

YOUR UNADORNED FACE

All the velocity
in the air between us wasted,
your grace, your unadorned face
has not sat down beside me.

I have the chair and the time.
Put on your smile, your fine
talk, plus our feathered meanings:
we can row backward
or, leaning close together,

row forward, meet tomorrow
with the years we can borrow
from our lively mutual knowing.
I see you small, and tall,
and always growing.

COMMENCEMENT

Most of us will never meet again
neither the gangling rose-armed girls
stammering on heels, white-shroud gowned,
their uninhabited hopes rolled up
in scrolls; nor one another's words, friends,
parents, brothers, our unused sighs spent
in this man-made tall-treed glen, leaf-light
and summer-drowned, designed for albums.

Oh, beginning of the beginning,
let them always walk to the muted
sound of horns, slowly, shy, but winning.

THE COLLECTOR

Daily the search continues,
knots of night are undone
to ravel up reality spun
from the nightmare's cryptic spell,
the locked door you walked through,
the look you left in the mirror.

Collectors can be savage,
obsessive, positive that you,
in your faultless, fashionable self
still walk slow up steep slopes,
over stones, through gates
opened and closed
for us, wanderers
through gates of one another.

Merely by your persuasive excess
I was disarmed:
I followed you then,
I will again.

CHURCH, ONE SUNDAY
AT DARIEN

The cat cornered a bird
the dog claimed he could talk.
You, my love, were there
in the church wall on your walk
through my mind.

You told the sea about logic,
me, about disgruntled dressmakers
long out of work; disconsolate,

they seized a cloud, gave it a fringe
all round, so that we could see
they had not forgotten their skills.

You thought to amuse me but
refused to give me back the
tale I had begun about you and me

and immortality.

THE LOVER IN THE HOUSE

The house reverberates, responds
to each hurried subconscious wish,
doors open, butter dances in its dish.
Lovers unlock hinges that stick.
Dark delivers the full moon tricks.
Wonder, longing, met and dispatched.
The landscape glows, becomes devout.
Reason was last seen checking out.

NO DOUBT

Whether it is a matter of pleasure
or the drops of time that part
the ordinary moment from the measured,
life is either vacuous
or an art.

III

ANTECEDENT

When Absalom hung by the hair
today's butterflies were there,
Hop-Merchant, Comma, Question Mark,
folded their wings to look like bark.
Giant Skippers held mating flights
at dusk. Admirals wore blue-green lights.
The bitter poisonous milkweed spun her
perfumed clusters when David's son
Absalom stole the hearts of men.
Butterflies knew no names then.

The long-haired sons of Absalom
break hearts and men.
Some wish them hanged.

THERE ARE THOSE

Punctuators make precise marks,
order genius and the fool alike,
plot the day, rewrite the dark,
forget no comma parts the night.

FOR A MASTER OF HIS CRAFT

What if we do read your reason,
words you taught, you taught them well.
You could even teach hostility
how to blow our willing minds.

Observation is on trial
raised to naked objectivity
lucidity now stands accused!
Could the jury of your peers
forgive the fury of your truth?

Has the judge put on the scarecrow's
tattered robes of the uncouth?
Hunted down by turgid phrases
headlines turned by flick of dial
must we settle, suck up soap flakes,
swap detergents and deodorants
for the patience of pure prose?

Is there still a time for reason
waiting in the land of fakes?

HEARTS IN THREE PARTS

Early on because of training
she took her good sensible shoes
and walked through life, discovering
Caesar was right, there were just three
landscapes in the kingdom of love:
animal, vulnerable and
miserable.

She made a map,
became famous. Her metaphors
turned into gold. Jingles were sung:
"Have you tried the shoe
that took her all the way through?"
When she died, her shoes cried.

THE LANGUAGE OF THE DEAD

Your silence locks me up,
takes shapes, lies about me visible
like colors in a shadow
that change when I go
to raise the shade of night
on one more saucer of light.

You left me with the snow
of absence all around me.
I have your touch, your hand
but cannot find you
in the red full moon.

I draw your walk, your gesture, face.
Your absence is the room
I cannot find the door for.

You whisper to me, more
to prove me wed to words
than to explain
why you have gone
or why I stumble through these rooms
that know your voice,
your secret place.

THE WINE OF ASTONISHMENT

I have counted all the threads
on a Queen-Anne's-lace face,
thorns on the first and last rose:
summer's sorcery winds and spins
her ropes of hope, her star-stitched carpets.

We worship her colors, her scene,
her perfect painted blooms.

Her secrets are secure, some day
she may divulge just why
we cannot read by the moon.

THE SEA SPEAKS

I am angry, not furious, just angry,
that thunder you hear came all the way from China:
too many places you will never see
guarantee my immortality.

When you were a child
I was frightening but fun,
you rode on my back but I
could throw you, make you cry
pails full of sand,
tears and fears.

I am the scripture, the lesson
no human can read,
both vengeful and just.
There is no King in my allegorical Kingdom,
Freud could not cure me
of my affair with the sun.

You will never tame my riches, my power,
I can turn your bones into coral,
I can kill, caress, I can rust.

Some jealous God has condemned me to lust
for the earthbound brown
of your fertile ground.

THE MONDAY MAN

The Connaught, London

There is a Monday man who comes
to wind the clock as pigeons knock.
Shy artisan, he winds his thumbs.
Clear toned, the proper clock responds.

His captive, I discover art
and habit co-exist, my heart
each Monday shall be wound. I'll strike,
bow clock men in and out, like life.

LETTER FROM THE DECEASED
WIVES OF HENRY VIII

Dear Henry, we trust you have found out
what royal heaven is all about,
and that the heart
is at least as important
as our fragile, favored other part.

You took our hearts and ate them whole,
wife to bed and knife to head.
Wooed and plundered, we surrendered
yet we pray to save your soul.

Henry, have you been forgiven?

TELEPHONE PAINS

The sun was doing her lattice work,
the amaryllis was ready for bursting,
the ficus stayed tall and indifferent.

I was dawdling with notes, definitions,
watching the monster, awaiting a ring.

Impatient, mad, the odious, obvious
instrument talked only to ambition,
hustlers on their feet
in the hurrying street.

A LITTLE ROMANCE

I stole you for that Venice shot.
Pigeons, bells and gilded domes—
what a picture-postcard site.

You would have collected the right
sources, Ruskin, Symonds, footnotes,
secrets of the city's past.
We would have made love to the sea

surrounding, with dusk in our eyes,
I would have gathered your image,
memorized Titians and bridges,
your way, your mood and the gold view

in its prison forever, would do
on nights when the silence talks.

THE SMALL SET

They do not know the names of trees, of seas, but mother's kiss
tastes very sweet when Dad looks pleased.

And how they run, up-down, flat-round, they run and never stop,
and they deceive, appease and tease, they're never mean.

And when they cry, they sob, they sob so far so steep and deep
and like the winter crocus, after long, closed-up sleep

they wake so radiant, proud, their colors oh so fair
we stop, we stare.

INTERRUPTIONS

Interruptions multiply without promise of purpose
the green light, the yellow, the red change.
It rains on what might have been said.

Eve was beguiled, the snake
interrupted her Eden.
Adam wanted Truth,
was given Reason!

LOUD LYRICS TO LINNAEUS

One bullfrog senior basso profundo
in harmony with his responsive bride
across the silence of a moon-hung night
in full throat and with permissible pride

sang: "We are the flood's direct descendants,
we talked of heresies leaving the ark,
redeemable pagans we shrugged at zealots,
our eyes could distinguish truth in the dark.

Tail-less leaping amphibians
made by the master ugly of face,
our hoarseness, my dear, was deliberate
so man might hear us croaking of grace."

THE LAW OF UNCONSCIOUS FALSIFICATION

When she was a girl she wanted
a voice, red hair and the choice
of all her suitors to be made by jury . . .
one had a night-blooming cereus
one a candy contract with the night operator
one had four hands
and one, sincere eyes—
the affliction of all lovers
who believe in themselves.

None of her small talents grew because
of their blandishments; she feared to choose,
feared her meticulous mother who locked her up
for this untidy habit. She refused.

At forty the games she played wore gloves.
Fear hid under the shibboleth tree.
She watched suckers strangle the bark, heard
pride cry in the dark. Doctors sighed,
refused to prescribe more make-believe,
the years multiplied what Freud described.

Continents she discovered forbade passports to pretense,
men became jugglers; flags up their sleeves

ceased to surprise. She learned to listen.
When there were words like mouths
She kissed them. She learned to steal.
Liberated, free to choose,
She found in each something sad and real.

A CONCLUSION

As nature unwinds her punctual days
our need to be rich with hours grows.
We heed the meaning of place,
undo distance, tear up mistakes,
accept the season's predictable ways,
garland a new truth with grace.

IV

EVERYONE'S WISH

If only we'd never doubted
Galileo's deductions and
Shakespeare's existence,
we might see through
to the heart of everyone's wish.

But none of us noticed,
we were too busy with truth.
When sea sounds woke Aphrodite,
we hammered speech into logic,

melted gods into gold,
wound words into watches,
wits into profits,
slaked thirst with false dreams.

The gods who color
the day and night
exactly as they like
weigh very light.

ABOUT MY FATHER

In each family museum
fathers wait to be called upon.
Mine in double-breasted buttoned blue
grace times height, heroic.
What questions, tests, defaults, did you
defy through sliding doors, through keys
and bolts? A ghost, you starred
in your own dreams, played pocket chess
against yourself, humped in chairs.

Now that you are long since dead,
I compose what you had never said.
A fabulist, you shook the humbug tree
of make-believe, wound up
life's toys for me.

You were vain, caught in mirrors bowing approval
at that high roman nose, those well-set eyes.
Women adored you, flimflam and all.
Girl children worshipped you,
you wore a wishing cap, times tall.

You broke all hearts.
Did your own beneath the well-pressed suits
know the ravelling stitch of failure?
Did you, in order to survive,

commute to fantasy and back?
Did you outwalk, outdance, outsham their taunts . . .
make me a world, where I would always be,
protected by the luck you promised me?

FOR DEIRDRE

I could get lost with you,
follow you into green dreams,
read you, brooding over destinations . . .

I can go backwards or forwards
in time, taking guesses
at your children's cream-colored voices,
like yours, rousing, rising, high-pitched
sounding like flutes, tuning up.

I see you in kitchens,
serious, pulled, struggling,
busy with the business of love,
squeezing the orange for a
morning-mated kiss.

Or I can go back to tow-head
devouring attention, filling rooms
with your babble, games, arms,
waiting to be caught with a kiss.

You will reach out to everyone
your battle won before begun.

VISITORS

Unexpected after the blizzard,
birds came nesting—computers
had recorded the advantageous location—
came and left, very small, and in their song
paid rent, praised the sheltering tree.
Their voice, translated by them
into hibernated secrets,
we could never share.

There was the air
that changed and the day that waited
for that silvery response from the sun.
Call it courtship, call it the musical overture,
the invitation to share and propagate
progeny. They sang before and during dawn,
impervious to the city's circus.

We could not read their wings
or why they aimed to this same tree,
while we changed plans, and walked
to nowhere, talking uninspired talk.

RUNNER ON THE RIDGE

You who jog North, think Greek
and you who swim South,
refuse the refuge of reason,
and we who stand light
on a carpet of dreams,
trust one another, recall
when we were alone
and that was all.

ABSENT FRIEND

Read us your Psalms
your selfless texts
your concise epistles
your untold deeds.

We have harnessed your wings
to a green tilted hill.
We have folded your heart,
the half you bequeathed us,
a bookmark for all your hopes.

All have been locked safe away
in the vault of your unravelled days.
We have mailed you the key.

FROM MY WINDOW

From the pointed, square church
arched upwards, clear, clean white,
bells sing out as if the heavens,
that promised unchartered nowheres,
opened a distant door.

My pine, attentive, listens,
shadows stretch out at their cue.
Branches sway, festooned arms swing,
applaud with the sun.

How tight we bind one another
in questions, appointments
plans for No and Yes, You-Me
and THEM. The day, meanwhile,
has moved the shadow's dial,

grasses, winds, gulls in formation,
perform their perfect pavane,
unaware of each other's motions
of you and me and our diurnal devotions.

ON THE PLANE

I left a yellow orchid
wearing a purple throat.
A jasmine hedge
waved me good-bye.
Why cry, I said to the car,
to the horrible hurrying
two-footed barbarous mob,
to the purposeless pushy queue.
Flapped wings flew their sail
on a rudderless boat.

The sky turned purple,
Braque and De Staël were outside
arranging their colors.
At sixty-five below in the snow
I was alone,
in an anonymous crowd,
going home.

THE LEGEND OF HIMSELF

His legs were longer than ours,
Country pride,
His need to challenge, helped him survive,
a man outside his size.

For forty years, between friend and foe,
under drying suns, sleeting northers,
between the first kiss and hovering oaks,
his schisms and his creeks rose.

Patience he renamed surrender,
reason he mined with homespun lore,
taught the wise outrageous laughter,
lessons they had not heard before.

The space he reached for hears him out:
he tells of skeptics, of false doubt.
His footfalls cast no sound;
young again, impatient still
he uses planets to persuade,
he sees the way we cannot see.

THE LONG WAY HOME

The Magi were never on my route
although I kept asking questions.
I really had no talent for covenants.

My greatest needs have been met
by reckless symbols; savage colors
brackish ponds that ate the saffron sky,
insatiable alps, ice-blue, snow-still
that stole the dusk's deep rose.

When I came to request an exchange
the queue was querulous and long.
They asked at the desk
for wisdom credit-cards
and I had none. I told them
I could still see color
in a barren tree.

All I possessed I confessed
was an armful of years,
undefined gifts
that could not be exchanged;
first green looks,
spring's audacious feathers.

I have known prophets
who wore salesman's ties,
sectarians who claimed
heavenly options;
I never believed either.
The way to Bethlehem for them
was written ritual.
But the color of the star,
though far, remains.

THE TIME KEEPER

Parse the nightingale,
he sings the night awake.
He is the lesser god,
nature's feathered infidel
whose tenor trembles
the porches of lovers.

Nothing he warbles
has meaning or thrust.
He knows neither saints, nor sorrow, nor sin.
He worships his own breath.
Nothing he sings of can rust.

LETTER TO MY SOUL

Since you are most likely to survive me,
you had better meet my gods
and know my predilections,
or have you been lurking and listening
between slumbers of your waiting seasons
for some latent virtue,
some random excellence,
to take a graft of my best shoots
to grow on the deciduous tree you tend?

Do choose a cherished city
for our everlasting winters.
Blocks of well-swept silence,
dogs and discreet neighbors,
scold the nervous horns.

Let the sun stop at open doorways,
let the voices of capable women
warm the treads of polished stairs,
let their heels tap out the rhythm,
let door and sill become a song,
Gregorian music,
tuned to desirable prayers.

Prepare dinners in textured brocade,
where the acorns of discourse
are passed on lichen salvers
to perceptive men and women,
their rustling reflected in mirrors
in the half-light of candles and arms.

No matter if sadness happens
no one could ever tire
of living up rivers of houses;
puberty practices scales,
old actresses polish antiques,
rich quarrels slam doors.
The evening chess game, under lamplight
planned to slake the thirst of argument,
overlooks envy and lust,
which winning or losing cannot checkmate.

PLACE DE LA CONCORDE

Ladies of Nantes, Strasbourg and Brest,
chaperones of cobblestones,
spreading your broad carved skirts you sit,
guardians of royal pleasance,

spending space where words have no weight
where lamps swing light into night,
dolphins disgorge their watery swords,

carrying the thrust of hurrying dusk.
Brim over, spill,
pour down, nubile nymphs

men have loved you, locked you in taste.
A king squared off his eyes' far reach,
the same Seine folds your corners west,

you sleep on iron pillows of park,
where heads once rolled to roll of drums,
blood still sings from gilt-capped palings.

High in the colonnaded arch,
starlings scold the feckless creatures,
selling favors for centuries more

than dukes put down for palaces.
The night smells of pulled-back drapes,
curious brocade, a view of grace.

A lion charges Marly's horse.
There was no limit, then, on space.

KATIE LOUCHHEIM has had two distinguished careers, as a public servant and as a writer.

She worked for the United Nations Relief and Rehabilitation Association after World War II, touring international relief camps in Germany. She played an active role in Democratic party politics, eventually serving as Vice-Chairman of the Democratic National Committee. From 1961 to 1967, she was the first woman to hold the post of Deputy Assistant Secretary of State. In 1968– 1969 she was American representative to UNESCO.

Mrs. Louchheim has published two previous collections of poems, *With or Without Roses* (1966) and *The Seeing Glass* (1979). She is the author of an autobiography, *By The Political Sea* (1970), and edited *The Making of the New Deal: The Insiders Speak* (1983).

The mother of two daughters, she lives in NewYork with her husband, Donald Klopfer.